HOMES
& GARDENS
L I B R A R Y   O F
I N T E R I O R S

Kitchens

HOMES
& GARDENS
LIBRARY OF
INTERIORS

Kitchens

Vinny Lee

PAVILION

To the Sweet Chef

First published in Great Britain in 1997 by
Pavilion Books Ltd
26 Upper Ground
London SE1 9PD

Text copyright © Vinny Lee 1997
Photographs copyright IPC Magazines Limited
except those listed below
Designed by Peter Bennett
Picture research by Kate Duffy

The moral right of the author has been asserted.

A CIP catalogue record for this book is available from the British Library.
ISBN: 1 85793 923 9

Typeset in Gill Sans Medium
Printed and bound in Spain by Bookprint

10 9 8 7 6 5 4 3 2 1

This book may be ordered by post direct from the publisher.
Please contact the Marketing Department.
But try your bookshop first.

Acknowledgements

The publisher should like to thank the following sources for providing the
photographs for this book:
Robert Harding Picture Library/IPC Magazines 29 bottom, 37
right, 40, 74 /**Jan Baldwin** 6 centre, 8 centre, 12 top, 19 left, 26 centre,
28 bottom, 36 top /**David Barrett** 78 bottom, 87 bottom /**Tim
Beddow** 32 top, 49, 73 left, 89 /**Geoffrey Bfrosh** 10 centre /**Dominic
Blackmore** 83 left /**Simon Brown** 26 top, 39, 46 centre, 50 right, 79
bottom, 91 /**Peter Cook** 11 centre /**Richard Davies** 75 /**Christopher
Drake** 7 top, 26 bottom, 29 centre, 33 bottom, 41, 45 bottom, 47 top,
48, 52 right, 60 top & centre, 61 bottom, 62 bottom, 66, 69, 71, 76 top,
77 top, 78 top, 81, 83 right, 85 left /**Michael Dunne** 78 centre, 84 /**Judy
Goldhill** 79 centre, 85 right /**Brian Harrison** 28 centre, 33 top /**Scott
Hawkins** 43 /**Lu Jeffery** 37 left /**Sheila Jones PR** 20 bottom /**Robin
Matthews** 8 top, 19 right, 46 bottom, 47 bottom, 52 left, 59, 61 top, 65,
86 /**James Merrell** 7 bottom, 13 centre, 21 right, 31 left, 36 bottom, 44
centre & bottom, 47 centre, 50 left, 55 top, 62 centre, 70, 72, 77 centre
/**Gwenan Murphy** 42 top /**David Parminter** 87 top /**Jonathan
Pilkington** 51, 54 left, 56, 67, 90 /**Trevor Richards** 7 centre, 11
bottom, 12 bottom, 13 top, 18 top, 21 left, 23 top, 24, 34, 35 top, 38, 45
centre, 57, 61 centre, 73 right, 76 centre, 80 /**Graham Seager** 27 top
/**Fritz von der Schulenburg** 6 bottom, 46 top /**Andreas von
Einsiedel** 6 top, 27 centre, 31 right, 32 bottom, 35 bottom, 42 bottom
/**Dean Wilcox** 25 top /**Polly Wreford** 12 centre, 18 bottom, 22, 58, 76
bottom, 82.
Arc Linea of Knightsbridge 13 bottom, 15 left, 23 bottom, 25 bottom,
55 bottom, 79 top, 88; **Brookmans Design Group** 44 top, 45 top, 54
right; **Bulthaup GmbH & Co** 14, 60 bottom, 64; **Chalon UK** 9;
Crabtree Kitchens 8 bottom, 10 bottom, 16, 62 bottom, 68; **Fourneaux
de France** 11 top, 20 top; **Hygrove Kitchens** 77 bottom; **McFadden
Cabinetmakers** 29 top, 30, 53; **A. Whale/Homes & Gardens
magazine** 10 top, 15 right.

Contents

Introduction

The kitchen is often referred to as the heart of the home — the friendly centre of a house, a room where family and friends gather, a place where food is stored, prepared and sometimes eaten.

These days most kitchens fulfil these roles and may expand on them, adding a laundry or sitting-room function. Some kitchens double as family dens or dining rooms; others are extended, due to the importance of their role in the home, and incorporate a conservatory or sun room.

Stylish kitchens have hidden depths, as not only do they look attractive but they must also be safe and hygienic. Fabrics, such as those used for curtains and chair covers, should be easy to remove and wash, as the build up of grease and stains caused by cooking will require them to be washed regularly. Easy-to-clean work-surfaces and floors, made of ceramic tiles, washable vinyl paint, linoleum and marble, with grouted or sealed edges to prevent

crumbs or bits of food from becoming lodged, are all important details of a clean and healthy scheme.

The increasing numbers of gadgets and labour-saving machines that are on offer also have to be fitted into the kitchen. To make these machines part of the overall scheme many are 'disguised' behind matching laminate or wood doors to make them appear as part of the kitchen. Easily accessible storage for the toaster, kettle and coffee machine can be created at the back of the work-surface, with a sliding glass or roll-top door to keep them at hand but neatly out of the way of flour and other cooking debris.

When planning a kitchen the first thing to do is work out where the main tasks will be performed – washing, cooking and storing; ie., where the sink, cooker and fridge will be fitted. In design terms this is referred to as the work triangle, as these three functions are usually performed in conjunction with each other, and should be within easy distance to save time and labour.

The location of the sink may be dictated by drainage outlets and plumbing requirements, so start with the sink, and then site the cooker and the fridge to be at the two other points of the triangle, so that you can work without

having to manoeuvre your way around an obstacle course of cupboards, stools and tables.

Once the basic plan is drawn then decide on the style of kitchen you would like. Traditional kitchens tend to be more ornate, often with wood – dark, natural or limed. The rustic look draws inspiration from the farmhouse kitchens of Europe, often using wood for units, as in the traditional kitchen, but with colourful washes of paint, bright blinds and curtains, and decorative hand-painted tiles.

The contemporary kitchen owes a lot to the professional kitchen. With an increasing interest in cooking and entertaining at home modern kitchens have turned to the equipment used in restaurants and hotels with large industrial ovens, grills and huge double-sized fridges. As in a professional kitchen, work-surfaces are kept clear when not in use, so in this style of design good storage and a large fridge are important.

Small kitchens require especially careful planning. Doubling up on functions can help recoup space; for example, a washing machine with integral dryer is two machines in one, a microwave that grills may replace a cooker, and a liquidizer with grinding facility could replace a couple of similar gadgets. Furniture that folds away will also save precious room.

In small kitchens ventilation is important because there is a limited area in which steam and condensation can disperse. An effective cooker extractor and a wall fan will help remove cooking smells, such as fish or curry, that may linger. Fans will also help prevent damp mould from forming by extracting moisture.

Whichever style of kitchen you choose, do ensure that the units and facilities such as the sink are at the right height for the people using it. If the units are low a tall person will experience backache from working in a stooped position, and conversely a short person will find it tiring to stretch up to a high surface.

Good lighting is vital in any kitchen. If adequate natural light is not available, additional electric lights will be needed, even during daylight hours. Work areas where potentially hazardous tasks such as cutting and slicing are performed, and places where hot dishes and fat or oil will be used, must be well illuminated to prevent accidents.

Another safety point to be aware of when planning a kitchen is the danger of sharp corners, on overhead units and extractor fans, as well as units. Either have these corners rounded, or sand or glass-paper them yourself or buy plastic corner caps that can be glued on with self-sticking pads. Of course, rugs and mats are best avoided in a kitchen as someone carrying a pan or kettle of hot water may slip and hurt themselves.

The kitchen may be a place full of potential hazards, but with adequate care and precautions it can be the place where a great deal of creative fun and family activity can take place.

Contemporary

Contemporary kitchens can be loosely divided into two categories – the updated classic and the new professional. In both cases the style is based on clean, unclut-tered lines and a light, fresh appearance.

Updated classic kitchens are mainly made of wood but

have modern details. Featureless doors, devoid of panelling or beading, with chrome comma or grab handles are common, and the use of pale or light woods with interesting grain are also popular.

Some of these kitchens draw inspiration from the past and re-interpret it with the use of up-to-date technology and materials. The pure, simple lines of the American Shaker furniture suits the minimalist ideology of the contem-porary kitchen, and the maple and black liner designs of Biedermier, from Germany in the early 1880s, can look as at home around microwave ovens and cappuccino makers as it did in the grand salon of a Hamburg house.

The simplest way to update a traditional kitchen is to change the unit fronts. If the lay-out of the exisiting kitchen is as you want it you could simply change the look by replac-ing all or some of the doors or by giving them a facelift. If you have standard wooden doors it may be possible to remove the beading and sand down the surface to remove the varnish or finish, giving you a fresh 'canvas' on which to decorate.

This canvas can then be coloured, cut into or otherwise altered. The unit fronts may be painted in a variety of different colours; choose two or three shades and invent your own scheme. Replace the knobs with modern

Kitchens

chrome designs, plain round wooden knobs painted in contrasting colours to the doors, or plain white ceramic knobs.

Cutting patterns out of the door itself can create an interesting effect, but cut the panel well within the outer edge, which is needed for support and sturdiness. Holes, circles or other patterns should be sanded to give smooth edges and then be backed with fine wire mesh or glass, to prevent dust and crumbs from getting into the cupboard. Removing the centre of the door and replacing it with a sheet of sandblasted or patterned glass will also give the kitchen a more contemporary look.

In the traditional kitchen plain glass may be found in the front of a dresser door, but in the contemporary kitchen glass becomes a feature. Sandblasted and etched with checkerboard designs or swirling wave-like patterns, glass gives a lighter and more interesting alternative to the soild unit door.

The laminate door has also come of age and is now available in a spectrum of interesting and unusual colours, in either a plain finish or with patterns. Instead of using one colour throughout for the units, there is now a trend to mix and match colours and designs.

The new professional kitchen comes straight from the realms of hotels and restaurants – it is chunky, business-like and mostly made from stainless steel. Free-standing steel work-stations have also been designed to emulate the professional kitchen, but on a smaller scale suitable for the average size of domestic setting.

A change in living space has also influenced the contemporary kitchen. For example, with the increase in open-plan and loft apartments the kitchen is often on show, very much a part of the main living rooms, so the style and design of the kitchen becomes increasingly important. These large open spaces will also accommodate the size and bulk of the professional-type units.

New materials such as polished resin, cement, slate, fake marble and MDF have given designers wider scope and seen a rise in the trend for using several materials instead of having a single finish throughout. The availablility of trims and accessories has also grown, and the modern kitchen may have two or three different, but compatible, handle designs, or just one long single rail across the whole of the front of the drawer or door.

Shapes for units and islands have also evolved. The contemporary kitchen does not adhere to the boxed, angular shapes of the traditional dresser and unit; instead there are oval work-stations, rounded unit fronts, even triangular-shaped cabinets. Large single sheets of steel can be cut and moulded to provide crack- and chink-free surfaces, creating sinks tops and work-tops that are easily wiped with a cloth or sponge. But care must be taken with steel as it may become scratched or gouged. Dents can be beaten out but only in areas where it is easy to get access. Special non-grit cream cleaners can be bought to use on these metal surfaces, and non-abrasive cloths and pads are better than wire wool or heavy nylon brushes.

The contemporary kitchen may appear cool and clinical but it can also can also be an effective yet streamlined family room, and the advantage of the uncluttered look is that not only are the surfaces easier to keep clean but other items such as stacks of cookery books, now in cupboards, will no longer accumulate a fine film of grease.

The showcase kitchen should be devoid of clutter, and well-planned units with pivoting internal shelves and racks mean that tins and utensils are easy and quick to reach, negating the need for leaving them out on the surfaces.

Clean surfaces in a family room are also an advantage as children are less likely to try and grab things, or pull

handles and flexes which could be dangerous, and the work-tops can provide a place on which to draw or do

homework when not in use for food preparation.

With the near-naked look of the extreme contemporary kitchen, plugs and sockets

are often fitted under worksurfaces or units, primarily so that they don't detract from

the crisp, clean lines of the design.

Instead of a splashback of conventional tiles the contemporary kitchen is far more likely

to have a mosaic of tiny tiles, a sheet of polished steel or a re-inforced glass back. Hand-painted and floral tiles are

definitely out of place in this type of kitchen. Flooring is similarly basic and often follows the industrial theme.

Polished and sealed slate, heavy-duty rubber tiles, linoleum and cement are all in keeping with contemporary

kitchen style. The hardness of the steel units can be softened by the addition of a wooden floor,

although the timber should be sealed to prevent staining.

Windows in this style of kitchen are usually shielded with blinds. Plain rollerblinds, fine-

slat louvres and even simple shutters will all suit this type of setting. If the windows are

overlooked or look out on an unpleasant view, replacing plain glass with frosted or opaque glass

will allow the light into the room while disguising the outlook. Features such as stools are very impor-

tant in a contemporary kitchen because, due to the lack of distracting clutter, each item that is on show is some-

thing on which the eye will focus. The curve and shape of the seat and line of the leg will

assume architectural significance in a minimalist setting.

There are hundreds of permutations between the new professional kitchen and the

updated classic category, and many ways to achieve a modern look with homely appeal.

The surfaces of this cool white and wood kitchen are kept clutter free and immaculately clean. These ideas are taken from professional environments which have inspired the modern style of domestic kitchen design. Skylights allow natural light to flood into the room but can be screened off by plain white canvas blinds. When cooking, lights under the upper units light the work-surfaces and in the evening a small halogen light over the table provides a focal point for dining.

As cooking smells can linger it is important to have adequate ventilation. A cooker hood with an extractor fan can make a big difference not only to the air quality in the room, but also to the amount of steam and condensation that builds up around the hob or cooker. Left: The conical steel hood is a smart way of making a utilitarian object into a feature. Right: The smoked glass hood appears lighter, less dominant and more in keeping with the painted brick walls than a metal version.

New surface finishes have brought a rainbow of colours and unusual details into the modern kitchen. Faux and reconstituted marble can be shaped and cut to give practical but attractive work-surfaces. Right: Draining grooves have been created in the work-top and, below, the end unit has an attractive rounded end which gives a softer feel to the kitchen. The mix of solid blue doors with pink geometric panels gives an eye-catching finish.

Left: Industrial finishes such as steel housing and grids enhance the business-like feel of the professional-style home kitchen. Laminates and veneers now come in a multitude of shades and can be mixed and matched to create a visually interesting scheme. Right: The doors under the sink are in a chestnut brown, those to the left are plum and the shelves are orange, yellow, blue and brown. Despite the mix of colours, the overall effect is unified and unusual.

Right: Seating in this kitchen is either on a cosy window bench or on bar stools at the oval work-island, which has an integral wooden chopping board. Family meals can be taken in comfort at the table, but snatched breakfasts and casual suppers can be eaten at the island. Below: A long, scrubbed pine table doubles as a place to mix ingredients and cook, and serves as a conventional dining area which can be dressed up with a cloth or left plain for relaxed meals.

Left: Loft or apartment dwellings are in vogue and these large, open-plan spaces often have a kitchen space that is an integral part of several other areas within the room. For example the dining, sitting and even balcony sleeping areas may all be in the one room, so effective lighting is especially important. Good ventilation is essential to avoid cooking smells lingering. Right: The double doors leading on to a small balcony give this upper-storey flat a light and open kitchen.

Right: Shaker-style tongue-and-groove boards have been used to create this simple kitchen. Although Shaker style dates from the eighteenth century, it is classic and fits well with the modern minimalist requirements. Below: This wood and yellow kitchen also uses traditional materials but the shapes, such as the boat like central work-station, and the use of etched glass in the doors give a contemporary feeling, while the colours add a sense of warmth and comfort.

Left: Detailing can really enhance plain units: here shapes have been cut out of the wooden cupboard doors to reveal a glass inset, and the work-station stand has been grooved to give a column-like appearance. The black work-tops also contrast dramatically with the two tones of wood used on the doors. Right: Although in an old building, the kitchen of this flat has a modern, simple and uncluttered appearance enhanced by the choice of angular contemporary stools.

Mixing old and new together can be very effective. Here the modern kitchen was designed around antique ceramic tiles from an old butcher's shop, with traditional polished-slate worktops on the units under the tiles. The contemporary steel handles, work-surface and mix of coloured-laminate finishes work well with the older elements. The juxtaposition of old and new is highlighted in the rest of the house: the building and its features are old, but the decor throughout is contemporary.

Top: Biedemeir style, like Shaker, comes from the past but is a classic that still has contemporary appeal. The contrast of light wood and black trim is strong and dramatic and can take the harder, uncompromising look of the uncluttered modern kitchen. Above: Again old and new have been combined; antique wrought-iron-work balcony rails and a central hanging arch contrast dramatically with the plain and neat surfaces of the main room.

This black work-surface gives a standard wooden unit a more contemporary appearance. The narrow, low shelf provides a display area for items that might otherwise have accumulated on the limited space below. The work-surface is also cut from a solid piece of material and runs smoothly around the sink. This provides an easy-to-clean, crack-free top which is more hygienic and less likely to collect crumbs and bits of food in recesses and joins.

25

Top: Small mosaic tiles and unit doors in a variety of shapes and sizes, but painted in the same pale wash, give this kitchen an unusual and contemporary appearance. Above: This spacious kitchen is light and simply decorated, which gives it a modern feel, but the warm, wood trim and floor prevent it from being too austere. Double steel doors, a large extractor fan and hood, and an array of steel cooking pans and utensils emphasize the professional-kitchen influence on this design.

Traditional Kit

The idea of the traditional kitchen owes much to its early roots when the kitchen was an integral part of the living area. The traditional kitchen is not just an area for food preparation and storage, it is one of the most important rooms in the house.

The look of the traditional kitchen is welcoming, earthy and often visually entertaining, with collections of china displayed on a dresser, decorative cermaic tiles, rows of spices and herbs, and pots and pans all on show. An accumulation of artefacts and kitchen equipment contributes to create this kitchen's distinctive appearance.

Traditional kitchens can echo previous styles such as Victorian, Edwardian, the 1930s, as well as old country farmhouse. Influences may also come from abroad and the sunny climes of the southern French region of Provence or the popular Italian area of Tuscany.

With Victorian gothic or Edwardian retrospective styles, old kitchen equipment such as copper pans and weighing scales will be mixed with their modern counterparts. The floors may be covered with a checkerboard pattern of black-and-white lino or stone tiles. Walls will be white or cream, with plain, square ceramic tiles.

Open shelves and dressers filled with soup tureens, chargers, plates and bowls, all reminiscent of the period they are set to evoke, will be surrounded by cookery books, ceramic jars for ingredients such as flour, barley and rice, and neat rows of utensils. To accentuate this period style plain white utilitarian china is most appropriate, and the

chens

fine bone china should be carefully stored away. These 'historic' kitchens are taken from the era of *Upstairs, Downstairs* in the grand houses where the kitchen was very much the servants' domain.

The classic English farmhouse kitchen is ideally situated in a good-sized room, with space to eat and entertain as well as cook. There should be an imposing stove at its centre, most likely to be a ceramic-faced Aga or Rayburn, fuelled these days by oil rather than coal. If the stove hasn't been fitted into the chimney breast then there may also be an open fire.

This type of kitchen, in its most authentic form, is less likely to be fitted, and will more probably be made up from a mix of old wooden cupboards, dressers, chests of drawers and tables. If the traditional kitchen is a modern interpretation with fitted units, these should have wooden doors in as near a natural finish as possible.

If the kitchen has a Shaker flavour – again this adaptable style can be used for a traditional country look with the right accessories and dressings – the units should be simply painted in an appropriate shade of greyish-blue or something similar. Plain fitted units can be given a Shaker finish by using the muted blue paint and adding a plain wooden work surface and simple wooden knobs.

The classic farmhouse kitchen has a large scrubbed wooden table at its centre where food is prepared as well as served. The floor is covered with a practical surface such as quarry tiles or polished wood. Walls may be clad in tongue-and-groove panelling or plain

plaster painted in crisp, bright white or a warmer shade of cream. Tiles are placed around the sink area and some-

times around the back of the stove.

Windows in the farmhouse kitchen are usually framed by decorative check or dainty floral curtains with a pel-

met, and if there is space it is an ideal place of a box- or window-seat – the typical place for the family dog or cat

to sleep in the sunshine. Even city kitchens and those in flats or apartments can be given

a more rural feel by planting window-boxes or pots with herbs or cottage-

garden flowers such as forget-me-nots and pansies, and fixing them

to the windowsill.

The essential accessories for the farmhouse kitchen include a dresser full of mix-

and-match painted china, a plethora of baskets, stoneware bottles and basins, and glass stor-

age jars filled with home-made preserves and pickles. A tablecloth of gingham check or freshly-laun-

dered cotton will smarten up the table for mealtimes and a mix of wicker- or rattan-seated wooden chairs will pro-

vide the seating.

A large ceramic Belfast sink with a wooden or slate draining-board, or even an original copper-clad pantry sink

and draining board, are ideal for the traditional kitchen. If you cannot find an original sink from a reclamation or

salvage outlet, there are a number of companies who make modern versions of the

ceramic sink. Copper sinks usually have to be specially made.

With Provençal and Tuscan styles there are subtle details that differentiate them from

the classic English farmhouse kitchen. Floors are most likely to be terracotta tiles or flags

with rush mats or hand-made rag rugs. The wall tiles will probably be hand-made, slightly uneven and brightly paint-

ed with birds or decorative designs. The units will be colour-washed, or old, well worn and characterful unpainted

wood.

The colours of these European kitchens revolve around the warm terracotta colour of the floor tiles and pottery, and the roughly-plastered walls which are usually white, although they may sometimes be sponged or ragged in Mediterranean shades of blue, yellow or apricot.

The essential accessories for these Continental kitchens are terracotta bowls, hand-painted cream and green

ware, wonderful plates and bowls painted with swirling circular designs and motifs in vivid shades of pink, yellow, blue and green on a white ceramic glaze, glass oil bottles, strings of dried chillis, sun-dried tomatoes, garlic, onions, bunches of drying herbs and two-handled urns.

At the windows of the Provençal kitchen there may be the typical French café curtains which cover the lower half or quarter of the window. These little 'modesty' curtains are often lacy, with pictorial scenes of birds, animals or windmills woven into them. Also evocative of the south of France are the Provence fabrics with small paisley-style motifs in strong red, yellow, green and blue colourways which add to the authentic look.

Both the French and Italian windows would traditionally be shielded from the midday sun and winter weather by full-length panelled shutters, either outside the house, or internal fold-away ones that fit neatly to the walls on either side of the window. Shutters are usually suitable for older houses but may look out of place in a more modern home.

Another influence on the traditional kitchen is the Scandanavian look, painted in soft Gustavian shades of silvery grey and pale powdery blue, with just a hint of aged gilt. Along with these cool colours are the decorative devices of simple wooden beading and panelling on cupboard doors.

The traditional kitchen covers a diverse range of inspirations from the past and from around the world. Whichever area or era you decide on, try to be as true to the style as you can, even if you do have to give shelf space to modern equipment and the microwave.

This kitchen has warm wooden units and a plethora of Mediterranean blue china with hand-made blue-white tiles and a wooden hanging rack. All these elements add to the homeliness and attractiveness of the kitchen. Yet the room is not overfussy or cluttered, it is functional, and has been carefully planned rather than left to evolve. This is a good example of a modern adaptation of a traditional style, suitable for a small terraced town dwelling rather than a large farmhouse.

To create the right tone, the details of a traditional kitchen are important. Left: A shaped and pleated pelmet covers the top of the curtains at the window but also finishes off the frame of the stable door. Hanging baskets suspended from the ceiling add to the appearance of a busy domestic setting. Right: A perennial favourite is the wooden dresser laden with china. Here, using a theme of blue-and-white china, the dresser provides a decorative as well as useful unit.

Green tiles have been used to different effect in these two kitchens. Right: This English-style kitchen has check curtains and three rows of plain green tiles used as a splashback to the sink. Below: The green tiles have been mixed with white and set in a diamond pattern which gives the whole wall a more decorative and continental feel. This has been enhanced by the use of terracotta floor tiles. Strategically placed green accessories such as bottles and vases help to unify the colour scheme.

Above: Terracotta tiles have been used as a covering for the wall behind the stove. These tiles, especially when roughly finished and uneven, tend to bring a traditional feel to most kitchens. Left: Floral cotton fabrics also evoke a country-style look. Florals mixed with gingham checks or plain fabrics, which echo one of the colours from the print, can be used to bring colour and pattern to a room otherwise decorated in a plain scheme.

This kitchen is so plain that it could almost be contemporary, but the accessories, such as the thick-top bench in the centre of the room, the copper jam pan and rooster tiles add a subtle country flavour. The abundant window box on the sill could be used to fill with herbs ready to harvest when the window is opened. A window box can make even the most metropolitan kitchen view seem a little more rural, and can be used to brighten up an unattractive outlook.

Above: A range is the most popular style of tradition-al kitchen stove, whether English, French or American in origin. Here a six-oven stove has pride of place, stacks of wood are kept in a recess and the stone flag floor is softened by a woven straw mat and a homely rag rug. Left: Don't forget the insides of cupboards. The white-painted tongue-and-groove panelling at the back of this cupboard makes a bright and fresh impact when the doors are opened.

Right: There is a 1930s period feel to this neat, cream kitchen. White utilitarian tiles have been used for the splashback behind the sink and open shelves with painted tins add to the atmosphere of austerity, appropriate to that time. Below: This kitchen is similar in size and shape to the one above, but has been decorated to give a completely different feel. Both are used as places to eat in as well as cook, but this room is country-style with plenty of strong colour and pattern.

Original features can be used to emphasize traditional style. Left: An old chimney breast has been kept as a decorative rather than functional part of the room. In some cases old fireplaces are used to accommodate stoves or cookers and ventilation pipes can be run up through the exisiting chimney. Both rooms have beamed ceilings in warm, honey tones, but in Tudoresque kitchens they may be painted black to resemble a pitch finish, or deep brown to look like oak.

This Shaker-style kitchen is simply decorated, but its clean, classic lines make it timeless. The peg rail around the top of the wall was used in Shaker dwellings to hang chairs and clothes on but here it has been used as an effective way of keeping utensils and crockery from cluttering up the work-top. Ample cupboard space also helps to keep work-surfaces clear. The grey-blue colour shown on the doors and rail is a typical Shaker shade; another authentic colour is a rich red.

The details in the kitchen below have been carefully thought through. The ceramic Belfast sink with brass lever taps gives a period feel. Old-fashioned brass weighing scales add to the look and butcher's hooks and chains suspending baskets of garlic and shallots endorse it still more. Yet the conveniences of modern life, such as a dishwasher, are incorporated into the scheme and become an integral part of the whole design without striking a jarring note.

This kitchen has a continental look. A French café-style half-curtain at the window obscures the view, yet lets light into the room, and the roughly paint-washed lower walls are in a rich Mediterranean blue while the upper half is in a crisp white – a combination of colours that is reminiscent of Greek island villages. Warmth is added with unpainted wood and the matching blind and tablecloth. The narrow plate rack on brackets above the door is an attractive way of displaying decorative china.

The gothic arch detail in the plaster frieze at the top of the wall has been used as a theme for the panels in the unit doors below. The diamond-shaped tiles also echo this chosen detail. It is often difficult to find a starting point when planning a kitchen but if you have an existing feature in the room, whether it be an interesting frieze or an unusual window, the shape of the motif may provide a source of inspiration for door design or the type of tiles you choose.

Right: The blank back of a unit has been painted with a *trompe l'oeil* picture of a dog resting on a blanket. This clever use of a plain panel makes it a feature of the room and a point of interest. A decorative motif has also made the extractor hood unusually eyecatching. Below: When not lit, this imposing stone fireplace could leave an empty hole in the middle of the wall but, by positioning a large wing-back chair in front of it, the fireplace frames the chair and the blank space is obscured.

This really is a French farmhouse kitchen but the design could comfortably grace a large kitchen in any home, even in the heart of the city. The tiled floor is practical and easy to clean, the range gives out plenty of heat and the dressers – one built-in on the right, the other a freestanding glass-fronted cabinet – supply ample storage. The old pine table and rail-back chairs provide a comfortable setting for family meals in a room where the furnishings are simple but pleasing to the eye.

Kitchens To Ea

Some rural cottage kitchens are still much as they were over a hundred years ago. The

open hearth may have been replaced by a stove, whether it is a Victorian

cast-iron version that requires blacking, or a more recent iron and

ceramic variety, such as an Aga or Belling; and water is now

supplied by pipes and taps rather than being carried in buckets from the nearby well,

although the cooking, eating and living functions all still take place in the one room.

   The contemporary open-plan living space in an apartment or flat also lends itself to this style of

multi-purpose area and in many modern homes the equivalent of this living/eating configuration can be seen in

kitchen/breakfast rooms, kitchen/diners and even kitchen/conservatories.

   The kitchen may be a traditional style with a long scrubbed-wood table that is used as an extra work-top during

food preparation, but then is cleared to be set as a family dining table. Children's meals and informal dining are well

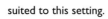

suited to this setting.

      Even in the modern kitchen with steel work-surfaces and professional equipment, a

central work-station or island can be cleared and set with china, cutlery and glass to pro-

vide a comfortable and attractive dining area.

   In some kitchens where more formal dining and entertaining may take place, a blind or partition may be used to

separate the working function from the entertaining side. A louvre slatted blind or decorative rollerblind can be

lowered from the ceiling to the top of the work-surface creating a temporary wall, which is easily raised again

In

when the kitchen is back in use. An old-fashioned hinged screen, or an Oriental wood and paper screen can also be used to create a 'mobile' wall.

In kitchens where more formal meals will be served it is important to ensure that the overall style of the room is adaptable to the two moods required. The room should be bright and airy to function as a practical kitchen, as well as smart and attractive to host a smart dinner party. Careful planning of colours and patterns will be important in the kitchen-cum-smart-dining area. There is no point in decorating this type of room in bright jolly gingham checks, and fruit and vegetable print wallpaper, and then expecting it to look chic for entertaining the boss to dinner. Schemes that will adapt to both uses could include traditional stylized floral designs or classic stripes with subtle and simple patterned wallpapers or plain painted walls.

For the kitchen that is used for informal dining the scope for decorating is much looser, but again try to think of the different moods you might want to create for various occasions and bear them in mind when working out your scheme.

Although very useful, and a liberating time-saver, machines such as the dishwasher, washing machine and microwave are not the most attractive things to look at. In a dual-purpose kitchen the outer doors of these machines might benefit from being covered with a fake door or panel that will make them blend in. The microwave could be concealed in a cupboard or upper part of a unit, or simply screened by a small curtain or panel. Here again *trompe*

l'oeil or clever paintwork could be used on doors to disguise the plain white metal covers of the machines.

Even the smallest details are important in a room like this where outsiders will be invited in. Small points that you might want to bear in mind are the taps and knobs, wastebins and even wall tiles, all of which will contribute to the overall look.

Tap fittings should be smart and in keeping with the style. If you have a Victorian-style kitchen you may go for an old-fashioned brass-effect fitting; if the kitchen is modern and sleek, then the industrial chrome lever-handle faucet is more appropriate. Door knobs on cupboards and units should also be chosen carefully. Even if the units or doors to which they are attached are plain, a stylish knob will lift the overall appearance.

Wastebins are an unattractive necessity, and if possible should be kept out of sight in a dark corner or in a cupboard; they should frequently be emptied and washed to prevent any unpleasant odours. Wall tiles are also important, as not only are they practical but they can contribute or detract from a scheme.

In a kitchen/diner it may be advisable to stick to a plainer design of tile for the majority of the wall, but to add a simple decorative border for pattern and colour. Too many patterned tiles will be overpowering, while tiles with a

kitchen theme such as chianti bottles or bunches of onions will only serve to remind the dinner guest that they are dining in the kitchen.

Although it is always important to keep a kitchen and its contents hygenic and clean, it is as important to be spic and span when you invite friends in to dine. They will see not only where they are going to eat but also where the food has been prepared; so make sure that the room and work surfaces are as clean and tidy as possible. Fabrics used for cushion covers and curtains should be easy-care and machine washable.

The same applies to floor and wall surfaces. Vinyl or washable wallpapers and paints are best in the kitchen, where steam and grease are likely to build up. Easy-to-wipe ceramic tiles are ideally used in areas around the cooker and sink, as well as behind worktops where slicing and mixing will take place and splashing is most likely to occur.

Sealed terracotta, stone tiles or linoleum are good, durable floor coverings that can quickly be brushed and

mopped, or sponged clean with soapy water. A butcher's rail or hanging rack is a useful way of keeping kitchen equipment to hand; but items that are only used once in a while will gather dust and grime, so these occasional-use implements may be best stored in a drawer, or else must be regularly washed to ensure their sparkling appearance.

In kitchens where meals are eaten the positioning and type of lighting is important. The lighting should be adaptable and adjustable as it may need to provide several different moods within the space of a few hours. The lighting must be bright and practical for safe and efficient food preparation and cooking. Under-unit lighting can be used to illuminate work-tops that extend under overhead cupboards, and directional ceiling spotlights can high-

47

light areas where it is important to be able to see clearly. For a more intimate atmosphere dimmer swiches and spotlights are useful, as are low-voltage wall lights or candles.

A clever idea that is worth incorporating in the kitchen/dining room is a double-sided cupboard. These units are attached to the wall by a side panel and have doors on both sides, front and back, so that plates, glasses etc. can be taken out and laid on the table from one side, but washed up and returned to the cupboard from the other. This type of cupboard also creates a useful room divider. Along the same lines are through drawers, which can be pulled out from either side of a unit.

The great advantage of the kitchen you eat in is that you are never far away from either your guests or where the food is being cooked.

When planning a kitchen where formal dining will take place it is important to plan the room carefully, down to the last detail. These elegant units have been finished with elaborate iron knobs and handles that are aesthetically pleasing instead of purely utilitarian. These small, but important, features will help to give the room a smarter appearance which will help when switching roles from bustling family kitchen to sophisticated dining area.

49

Carefully thought-out details add character to this eating area. The doors and drawers on the lower half of the dresser have decorative brass handles, which add interest to an expanse of warm yellow paint, as does the cut-out edging below the cupboards. Glass protects the crockery from acquiring a film of dust and grease. The narrow, worn wood table gives the room a lived-in feel, and cushions add comfort to garden-style benches. A tiny mirror reflects the wall light back into the room.

Less formal dining areas in kitchens can be set up using an existing kitchen table, some foldaway chairs and a cotton cloth. Eating in the kitchen has the advantage that the cook is not separated from the guests and that tricky dishes such as soufflés and flambés can be served immediately they are taken from the oven. The disadvantages are that culinary disasters will be witnessed by those waiting to eat and that the kitchen should be kept tidy as it is on view.

51

Opening up a large doorway between two rooms has created an informal kitchen-cum-dining room. Country-style checks and a traditional stove – which also heats the room – combine with a contemporary colour-wash on the tongue-and-groove panelling to create an unusual-looking room. The original flooring from the two rooms makes an unobtrusive division between the cooking and eating areas, and natural materials add warmth to the cool green-and-cream scheme.

The arrangement of a dining area within a kitchen is important; there must be space enough for people to get in and out and to ensure that no one is sitting perilously close to boiling pots or hot oven doors. Above right: The table is separated from the cooking areas by a unit, and the tiled splashback of the kitchen gives way to painted walls in the dining area. Above left: An outdoor theme and colouring gives the impression of space in a small room.

This double-sided unit divides the cooking and dining areas. Subtle changes in lighting can alter the eating area with its high stools from a brightly lit breakfast bar to an area more suitable for a quiet lunch or supper. One side of the unit accommodates the seating while the other provides storage space. The entire top can be used as working space if necessary, and the design means that there is barely a distinction between the cooking and eating areas, providing a truly dual-purpose room.

Creating a focus can be a way of attracting the eye away from other less attractive parts of the room. Left: A store cupboard door has been painted with a *trompe l'oeil* to make it look as though it is a dresser filled with interesting china, books and knick-knacks. Above: The central feature of this room is the island unit which has been painted in dark green in contrast to the light yellow and white used elsewhere. The border on the floor round the unit also helps to attract the eye.

55

Lighting is important is a dual purpose room. Good, bright lights are needed when the kitchen is used for food preparation and cooking but, when a cosy supper is being eaten, lights should be dimmed or varied to create a comfortable and relaxing environment. Top: Spotlights over the sink and table can be turned up or down as needed. Above: Daylight from the windows will fade as the day passes and additional electric lights will be needed.

The units in both the kitchen and dining areas are the same, which gives a feeling of unity and space to a small room and makes the dining area appear as an integral part of the kitchen rather than an afterthought or later addition. Even the table has the same fine, dark, wood inlay design as the unit doors and panels over the cooker hood and the ceramic tiles have been chosen to blend rather than contrast with the scheme. A skylight allows extra light into the windowless side of the room.

This round table is well positioned to allow easy access to the work areas around the edge of the room. The overall decoration of this kitchen is light and not overpoweringly kitchen themed. The ceramic tiles are bright but neutral in design and the fresh gingham blinds give an unfussy but finished appearance to the windows. Padded cushions make the chairs comfortable to sit on and the blue and white fabric with yellow piping matches the main scheme.

An old wood dresser base has been used to provide a barrier between the kitchen and dining areas of this kitchen. The drawers and cupboards face the dining room so that cutlery and linens can be easily stored but the top is accessible from both sides and can be used as an additional work-surface in the kitchen when needed. Under the unit on the far wall the shelves have been covered by a curtain instead of doors, which adds to the country feel.

A raised platform separates the kitchen and eating areas. The flooring and soft green paintwork have been kept the same throughout, unifying the room's functions. This open area is ideal for a family with small children as an adult working in the kitchen will be able to keep an eye on babies and toddlers elsewhere in the room. The chequerboard lino tiles are hardwearing and easy to clean which make them a good choice for a busy thoroughfare.

Kitchens To Re

With the increasingly important role that the kitchen plays in modern homes many ancillary functions have joined the primary ones of cooking and eating. Families with young children often find that the kitchen is the centre of social activity and doubles as a playroom. It is an area where adults can unload the washing machine or boil the kettle while still keeping an eye on their children.

Friends may drop in with their children and join in playtime in the kitchen, rather than disturb the sitting room. The kitchen, with its easy-to-wipe surfaces, is probably the best room for budding young artists to express their love of coloured paints and crayons, and for junior racing aces to rev up their high-speed plastic racing cars. Spills and accidents can be more easily mopped up from a linoleum or tiled floor than a carpet, and tiles and vinyl painted walls are more easily cleaned than those decorated with wallpaper.

In the kitchen that doubles as playroom or room in which the family relax, adequate safety precautions are important. If young children are playing anywhere near the work-surfaces it is vital that corners are rounded or capped, and that there is a safety guard around the hob so that little hands cannot grab hold of sauce- or frying-pan handles. Drawers and cupboards that contain sharp implements or knives and harmful liquids such as detergents and bleach should be fitted with safety catches or magnetic clips.

If the kitchen is L-shaped or has a breakfast bar or island, it may be possible to fit a safety gate to separate the

ax In

playing area from the cooking, keeping babies and toddlers well away from hot pans and boiling water, but still in clear view.

In a room where there are so many potential hazards it is wise to have a fire extinguisher and fireblanket to hand. Your local fire prevention or safety officer will be able to advise you on the best ways to protect you and your family.

Kitchens are often the family pets' room too. Dog and cat baskets or rugs, water and food bowls and their favourite toys may also need space. Flaps installed into the back door will give pets easy access to the garden, but it is often best to get a collar with a magnetic device that triggers one in the flap, only admitting your family pet and keeping out strays that may make their way into your home.

If you have a TV in your kichen, it needs to be accommodated in a way that will protect it from damp and steam but leave it clearly visible to those who want to view. This problem can be solved by putting the TV into a unit that matches the rest of the kitchen fittings; but the unit must be well ventilated, by drilled holes or a wire mesh insert, to allow the heat of the television to escape. Wall brackets are also useful for supporting a TV; the metal brackets are secured to the wall – therefore not taking up valuable work-surface – and can be pulled out so that the TV is clearly visible when needed, or pushed back out of the way when not required.

As kitchens are often at the back of a house it is usually the easiest room to extend, whether to add brick walls and a tiled roof or simply to open out the back wall into a conservatory. These additional rooms or extensions add to the space of the kitchen, and may include a table and

chairs or a sofa and easy chairs in which to relax.

If your kitchen extends into a conservatory it is worth taking time over planning for the seasonal changes that

you will encounter. If the room is to be in regular use it is worth considering the option of a double-glazed room

which will give you better insulation than single-glass walls. You can fit a number of radi-

ators to the solid walls of the room, or even install underfloor heating

when the foundations for the conservatory are laid. There will also

be a certain amount of heat from the cooker and hob when

in use. In the summer the problem will be getting rid of the heat and cutting down on

the sun's glare and bleaching effect which will make fabrics in the room fade. Good blinds will

help to reduce both glare and heat, and the same blinds, with special reflective backing, may also

insulate the room in winter. Special heat-sensitive devices can be attached to windows so that they automatically

open when the temperature rises above a certain point. These are useful for roof-lights, but for security reasons

are not advisable on lower windows.

A conservatory kitchen or extension has the advantage of being full of light even on the coldest of days, and

gives a feeling of space and airiness that cannot be re-created inside four brick walls or

under a slate or tile roof. The ample light provided by a roof-light window or glass con-

servatory roof is useful in a working kitchen environment.

Heating in kitchens is often a problem as you do not want to sacrifice valuable wall

space where units and cupboards could be placed to site a radiator. Modern slimline heaters are effective, and lad-

der radiators that double as towel rails can be fitted vertically up a wall, taking up the minimal amount of space and

providing a useful place to dry out tea towels and cloths.

The kitchen is often a room that heats up quickly when pans are boiling, and the stove, washing machine and

dishwasher are all in constant use, so it is equally important to be able to air the room and reduce the tempera-

ture. The extractor unit over a hob will remove a substantial amount of heat as well as cooking smells from that

area, and specially-fitted ducts will take the damp and steam from the washing machine and tumble drier out of the

kitchen. Small extractor fans fitted into windows or walls will add to the efficient reduc-

tion of heat.

For the decoration of a kitchen-cum-family room, it is worth bearing in mind the sort

of treatment and wear and tear that the surfaces will have to tolerate. If you have small

children go for tough and durable finishes. If you opt for plain vinyl-painted walls and a sensible washable tile floor

covering, by using bright or pretty decorative fabrics for blinds, curtains, laminated and wipeable tablecloths and

seat cushions, you can create a warm and welcoming scheme. Walls can be decorated with a useful cork or felt-

covered pinboard which can be used to display family photographs, school memorandums, party invita-

tions and samples of the children's handiwork.

For adult-only households the kitchen-cum-conservatory or room to relax in can be

decorated with less emphasis on the durable, although the effects of steam and cooking

should be kept in mind.

The kitchen area can be linked to the lounging or relaxing area and the two purposes can be differ-

entiated by use of different but harmonious colours and patterns, joining the two rooms, but providing two distinct

moods.

Kitchens to relax in are growing in number and size, and many manufacturers are pay-

ing heed to the demand for units and dressers that also have an informal living-room

charm.

This modern, open-plan room combines a well-lit kitchen with a relaxing sitting area. The wall of windows fills the room with light and makes it seem bigger and more spacious. Two wicker easy chairs and a chrome-and-leather armchair are placed on either side of a small fireplace, and two tables provide a resting place for coffee cups and magazines. The use of a deep terracotta and black scheme adds warmth and depth to what might otherwise be a cold room.

Two smaller rooms were knocked through to form a larger family area with kitchen. The same colours, and tongue-and-groove-effect panelling as the kitchen units (detail, right), have been used on the cupboard that stores the children's toys and games. The table doubles as a desk and drawing table where homework and 'works of art' are created. With this open-plan layout an adult can do domestic chores while keeping an eye on younger members of the family.

Relaxing on a day bed next to the stove sounds like the perfect way to spend a winter's evening. The daybed and small armchair do not get in the way of the oven doors so don't hinder its primary purpose, but the furniture is grouped around it as though it were a fireplace. This recalls old rural homes, where the kitchen was the main room of the house and a set-up similar to this would have been common. A mix and match of fabrics adds to the homeliness.

The room has been knocked through and extended with a conservatory-style glass ceiling, creating a large open-plan space. On the far side easy chairs provide a place to relax and watch television, the nearside area is furnished with a generously sized table and chairs for dining and around the edge are worktop and cooking facilities. The glass-fronted units have small curtains to screen the contents of the cupboards and give a more finished look to the scheme.

A glass roof-panel makes this small kitchen light and airy and a welcoming place to spend time. The decoration is simple and understated which makes it less obviously a kitchen and more acceptable as part of a larger room with other functions. The lighting over the sink, preparation and cooking areas is from recessed spotlights, but over the table neat suspended ceiling lights with shades have been used to give a more formal and decorative appearance.

Turning the back of the sofa to the dining and kitchen areas allows it to act as an informal barrier between the eating and work areas of the room and the relaxing section. Plain wood and brick provide a backdrop to more decorative features: the upholstery on the sofa compliments the ornate patterns on the Victorian-style tiles used in the far corner of the kitchen. Plain scatter cushions pick up the main colours of the fabric and are tied using ribbons made from the same material as the sofa.

This family room is used for preparing and cooking food as well as a place where meals are eaten. By filling a noticeboard with hundreds of postcards and using a plate-rack to display handpainted ceramic plates, the emphasis on decoration has been diverted from a wholly kitchen theme to a more general living-room scheme. The rug in front of the Aga softens the floor, but should be well secured so that it doesn't cause someone to trip or stumble when carrying food to or from the stove.

This dual-purpose room has been cleverly decorated to make it feel less of a work space and more of a room. For example, the glass panels of the cupboard door have been lined with fabric that matches the blind, concealing the contents and giving a finished appearance. Cookery books have been lined up on a shelf, like a small library, and a row of pretty china mugs are displayed on hooks beneath the shelf, keeping the worksurface free and tidy.

A built-in bench provides a permanent seating area in the narrow, galley-style kitchen. The apricot and sage colour scheme is both restful and warm and a multi-coloured runner on the floor – which should be carefully secured for safety reasons – makes the tiled floor warmer and softer underfoot, all important considerations in a room for relaxing in. The soft fabric lampshade will also give a diffuse orange glow to the light, creating a mellow atmosphere.

Left: Because kitchens are generally at the back of the house, a conservatory-style extension can be an appropriate way of enlarging the room. This sort of extension needs careful planning because it could be cold in winter unless double glazed and heated, yet unbearably hot in summer if not well aired and shielded by blinds. Above: A welcoming atmosphere imbues this kitchen, thanks to the brightly painted shelves housing an eclectic mix of toys, books and ornaments.

The flue for the Aga has been cleverly disguised in what appears to be a timber beam supporting the metal hanging frame with chillies and herbs. The change in flooring and the back of the Aga act as a divider between the kitchen area and the family room where two well-upholstered sofas offer a place to gather and relax. A set of decorative shelves with a display of blue-and-white china emphasize the fact that the seating area is still closely connected to the kitchen.

This small room has been cleverly divided to perform three functions. The sofa in the foreground is the 'sitting room', the dining table can double as an extra work-surface and the kitchen function is fulfilled by the units along the back wall. The black-and-white tiled border around the splashback is picked up by the linoleum floor tiles and the tablecloth. The vivid blue walls throughout are fresh, clean and bright, making the room appear spacious rather than claustrophobic.

Small Kitchens

To make the best use of a small kitchen requires discipline and careful planning. Take inspiration from other similar small spaces; think of a ship's galley or a car-avan where everything has its place.

To start, ask yourself some simple questions: from your answers you will be able to deduce the sort of equipment you need. Begin with the cooking facilities. What sort of cook are you? Will an electric frying pan and a toaster suffice? Is a microwave more suitable for your purposes than a cooker? Do you eat out a lot and live on soup and sandwiches when in, or dial for a pizza?

To gauge the fridge size answer the following. Do you live near shops and pick up food and supplies on a regular basis, and so can make do with a small fridge? Or do you live miles away from shops and work erratic hours, which means you shop once a week and need a large fridge as a store? By really studying the type of cook you are and

the lifestyle you lead, you can whittle down the kitchen equipment and fittings to a basic but useful minimum.

Also think about doubling up; see if you can get gadgets and units that have more than one use. For example, a microwave that browns may negate the need for a grill. A chop-ping board that slides over sink or draining area provides an extra worksurface. A stacking steamer means you can cook two or three vegetables at once. A waste compactor or disposal unit means less rubbish to find bin space for, and a blender/juicer will provide two machines in one.

When it comes to crockery and china, think along the same lines as the questions asked about fixtures and fittings; eliminate everything but the essentials. If your whole flat is small, how many people would you entertain? If the answer is six at the most, then have six plates, bowls, knives, forks, glasses, etc. Give away odd plates and bowls and dishes that may be useful 'someday'.

The same rules apply to furniture. A drop-leaf folding table will provide a dining area or extra work surface when needed, but fold flat against the wall and out of the way when not. Folding chairs can be stacked away in a cup-board or another room. A trestle table is another useful device, as the flat top can be slipped under a bed and the foldaway leg sections neatly concealed until needed. A stepladder that folds into a stool can also be useful, especially if you use the out-of-reach tops of fitted units to store things that are less frequently used.

There are many types of internal baskets, and rotating and adjustable shelves that make the maximum use of space inside fitted units. Narrow sliding shelves can fit at right angles between two upright units, revolving circular wire shelves can be used in difficult corners, and adjustable shelves can be altered to accommodate different sized jars and boxes. Boxes that stack on top of one another can be used to fill a shelf space from top to bottom, and to make finding their contents easier; good clear labelling will save a lot of time and effort.

To utilize every inch of space think above and beyond the work-surfaces. A plate rack

over the sink, fixed between two units, will provide a handy place to keep china as well as an ideal area for plates

to drip-dry after washing. Hanging rails or old butcher's racks can be secured to the ceiling and used to store larger

and more frequently-used items. These are useful in freeing up drawer space for smaller items. But don't have too

much equipment hanging around as, in a small kitchen, you may bump into it and find that all the clutter hanging

about the place makes a tiny room feel even smaller.

Create the illusion of space by keeping work-surfaces as clear as possi-

ble. Reinforced glass shelving is light and almost invisible, which also

creates a feeling of room. Glass shelves in front of a window

will provide extra storage but still allow light to come into the room. As a feature like

this will tend to be eye-catching do make sure that the items on the shelves are worthy of

viewing; no half-empty jars of tomato sauce with dribbles or half-eaten packets of biscuits.

Doing away with standard wood, laminate or MDF unit doors can also provide a few extra precious inches.

Instead of a rigid door, a soft curtain of fabric or an adapted plastic shower curtain will conceal the contents of the

unit or shelves behind, but allow extra space for knees and feet while standing in front of it.

There are many ways of creating a partition between the two functions of a room, but in the case of the small

kitchen the partition needs to be useful as well as decorative. For example, a bookcase

may work well as its back could act as a splashback to the sink, and the shelf side, filled

with china and glass, would provide storage as well as a decorative addition to a dining

area. A simple folding screen can also provide a temporary wall.

Built-in seats are another way of conserving space in a kitchen/diner. Two benches can be built along adjoining

right-angle walls. The base of the benches could be designed with a hinged seat or under-seat doors to provide

additional storage space for pots and pans. A table can be pushed up neatly against the benches when not in use.

A window is a great help in a small kitchen as it prevents a claustrophobic atmosphere by giving a feeling of space beyond and by allowing daylight into the room. If you don't have an outside wall for a window, investigate the possibility of putting in a sky- or roof-light, or even paint a fake *trompe l'oeil* window on to a wall.`

Make use of every surface, nook and cranny in a small kitchen. Use the back of the door for a noticeboard for

shopping lists and notes. A butcher's block on wheels can give extra surface area but is easily rolled out of the way or into a corner when no longer needed. Hanging net bags inside a cupboard door to store vegetables or dried goods such as packets of lentils or beans is a way of using even the smallest gap between the door and the shelves.

If your kitchen is very cramped try to keep cleaning and laundry items in other rooms and use the kitchen solely for food and its preparation. For example, you could install a washing machine/tumble drier in the bathroom where you will already have the right plumbing facilities, drainage and ventilation.

When decorating a small kitchen the best rule is to keep it bright, light, simple and fresh. A small

room will feel even smaller and darker if you use a deep, dark colour or a heavily patterned wall-paper or similar-style ceramic tiles. Mirrors, used as splashbacks, or a polished steel back to a cooker will help reflect light back into the room, and create a feeling of space. Glass fronts on wall-mounted upper units will be lighter than solid doors. Plain, large ceramic tiles rather than small busily-decorated ones will also help create an illusion of space.

If you add a dado rail a few inches from the ceiling join and paint the area above the dado and the ceiling white it will make the ceiling seem taller. Vertical stripes, whether painted on to the walls or on a wallpaper, will also help give height to the room. Concealed lighting hidden inside the top rim of the tallest wall-mounted units and pointed up to the ceiling is another trick that can fool the eye.

Hanging racks suspended from the ceiling can be a good way of gaining space in a small kitchen. Do make sure that they are sufficiently high, or placed in an area above a unit where you don't need much access – to avoid hitting your head on the hanging pots and pans. The plate rack above the sink doubles as a drainer as well as storage. Try to double up on functions in a room where space is limited. Here, careful planning and plain white walls help to achieve a feeling of space.

In a small kitchen a unit like this could be fitted in between two doorways, in an area that might otherwise be classified as 'dead' space. Instead of making the whole unit as continuous cupboards, two small areas of granite work-top, illuminated by concealed lighting, have been incorporated, which can be useful if that sort of space is scarce elsewhere in the room. French doors also help to bring light into the room and should be left uncur-tained if possible, to maximize natural light.

In this small, narrow kitchen a Shaker-style peg rail is used to hang chairs out of the way when the dining area is not in use. A plate rack over the sink provides neat storage for crockery, and the gothic shape of the narrow, glassed panels in the doors on either side help to give an illusion of height and space at the end of the room. Bright white paintwork makes the room clean and fresh and the wooden work surfaces and coloured tiles add warmth and character.

Storage is important in a small kitchen. Left: These glass shelves provide useful surface areas but appear light and insubstantial. Shelves like these should be made from special reinforced glass that is stronger than normal glass and will not splinter into shards if broken. Right: A pantry cupboard with spice racks built into the doors and wicker vegetable baskets beneath also has a small area of worktop, making maximum use of a limited area.

Although the windows in this kitchen are small and at the top of the wall, they do give a certain amount of daylight, and ventilation when necessary. The area on the wall under the windows has been used to hang a decorative display of baskets. The light colour scheme of white and yellow helps to give a feeling of space and the use of small rounded knobs on the unit doors will help avoid using up valuable room and be kinder on your legs if you bump against them.

The advantage of a small kitchen is that you may choose to use expensive tiles or wallpaper that in a larger kitchen may be too costly to consider. Above left: This attic room has been decorated with dramatic black-and-white wallaper and tiles that create an impact. Above: In this simply but stylishly decorated setting the fine slat blinds are eyecatching because of their colour and texture. Blinds are useful where you need to save space because they fit neatly to the window.

This conservatory kitchen has a central unit which doubles as a work area and a dining table. High stools provide a perch, but can be neatly tucked away under the unit when not in use. The plate rack over the sink saves space and energy, and patterned glass in the cupboard doors makes them appear less solid but keeps the contents obscured from view. Light from the glass ceiling above makes the room bright, but blinds can be pulled over to reduce glare.

Above: Blinds and shutters are useful window dressings in a small kitchen because they take up less space than the pleats and folds of pulled-back curtains. Blinds are especially good when used behind a sink because they can be pulled up out of the way of splashes and detergents when the sink is in use, and lowered again when needed. Left: a curtain conceals the shelves beneath this unit and is a softer, less rigid alternative to a wood or laminate door.

Try to tailor a small kitchen to suit your lifestyle. If you don't enjoy cooking a microwave may be a better choice than a full-sized cooker, and if you eat out a lot a small under-unit fridge may be all you need to hold breakfast or occasional supplies. A roll-top door can be brought down to cover this section of kitchen shelves and is more space saving than opening standard unit doors. The roll-down door will also give a neat, uniform finish, flush with the wall.

Long, narrow rooms are often referred to as galley kitchens, like those on a ship. Units running along both walls will provide storage and work-surfaces. The advantage of this type of small kitchen is that you don't have to walk too far to gather ingredients, prepare and cook them – everything is to hand. The use of white tiles and walls helps with the illusion of light and space and the emerald green units are simple and unfussy in design, avoiding a cluttered look.

This attic kitchen is simple and plain in design and colour scheme but a small porthole mirror on the wall may be a humorous allusion to the fact that the space is as small as a boat's galley. The window treatment is also cleverly devised to take up a minimal amount of space. The long pelmet frames the window and a roller blind has been fitted to run inside it. The bright-green check of the material and the unusual shape focuses attention on the window.

Raising the ceiling can be a way of gaining precious inches in a small kitchen and if there are no windows or access to daylight, removing the ceiling and going up into the beams may provide an opportunity to install a roof light or glass panel. Here the extra inches retrieved amongst the rafters have been used to provide storage space on top of cupboards and the beams themselves are a perch for a pair of decoy ducks. An additional shelf has been tucked between the unit top and cupboards.

Directory

UNITS

Andrew Macintosh Furniture, 462/464 Chiswick High Road, London, W4 5TT. Tel. 0181-995 8333. Simple classic designs.

Arc Linea of Knightsbridge, 164 Brompton Road, London, SW3 1HW. Tel. 0171-581 2271. Free-standing and modern designs.

Brookmans, Fairholme Works, Jawbone Hill, Oughti-bridge, Sheffield, S30 3HN. Tel. 01742-862011. By appointment only.

Bulthaup, 37 Wigmore Street, London, W1H 9LD. Tel. 0171-495 3663. Ultra-modern and streamlined designs.

C P Hart, Newnham Terrace, Hercules Road, London, SE1 7DR. Tel. 0171-902 1000.

Crabtree Kitchens, The Twickenham Centre, Norcutt Road, Twickenham, Middx, TW2 6SR. Tel. 0181-755 1121. Traditional and Shaker-style kitchens.

Hayloft Woodwork, 3 Bond Street, Chiswick, London, W4 1QZ. Tel. 0181-747 3510

Hygrove Kitchens, 152/154 Merton Road, London, SW19 1EH. Tel. 0181-543 1200. Traditional and modern classic designs.

Ikea, Tel. 0181-208 5600 for nearest stockists. Wide range of self-assembly kitchens in classic and modern styles.

John Lewis of Hungerford, Park Street, Hungerford, Berks, RG17 0EA. Tel. 01488-682066.

Just Kitchens, 242/244 Fulham Road, London, SW10 9NA. Tel. 0171-351 1616.

Magnet, Freephone 0800 555835 for stockists. Wide range of economically priced styles.

Mark Wilkinson, Overton House, High Street, Bromham, Nr Chippenham, Wilts, SN15 2HA. Tel.

01380 850004. Showrooms also at 126 Holland Park Avenue, London, W11 4JA. Tel. 0171-727 5814; 41 St John's Wood High Street, London, NW8 7NJ. Tel. 0171-586 9579; 13 Holywell Hill, St Albans, Herts, AL1 1EZ. Tel. 01727-840975; 4 High Street, Maidenhead, Berks, SL6 1QJ. Tel. 01628-777622; 17 King Street, Knutsford, Cheshire, WA16 6DW. Tel. 01565-650800.

Miele, Fairacres, Marcham Road, Abingdon, Oxon OX14 1TW. Tel. 01235-554455. Contemporary and traditional styles of kitchens.

Newcastle Furniture Company, 128 Walham Green Court, Moore Park Road, London, SW6 4DG. Tel. 0171-386 9203.

Noname by Capricorn, Capricorn House, Birchall Street, Liverpool, L20 8PD. Tel. 0151-933 9633. Modern stylish designs.

Plain English Cupboard Makers, The Tannery Combs, Stowmarket, Suffolk, IP14 2EN. Tel. 01449-774028.

Poggenphol, Tel. 01908-606886 for stockists. Modern as well as Shaker-inspired kitchens.

Rhode Design, 65 Cross Street, London, N1 2BB. Tel. 0171-354 9933. Simple but beautifully-made kitchens with etched-glass panels and subtle choices of colour.

Robinson & Cornish, Southay House, Oakwood Close, Roundswell, Barnstaple, Devon, EX31 3NJ. Tel. 01271-329300. Traditional style.

Shaker, Tel. 0171-724 7672, or **Plain English Cupboard Makers,** Tel. 01449-774028. The original Shaker company now making kitchens.

Siematic Kitchen Designs, Tel. 01438-749780 for stockists. Modern and traditional styles.

Smallbone of Devises, 105–109 Fulham Road, London, SW3 6RL. Tel. 0171-589 5998. Other showrooms in Knutsford, Devises, Harrogate, Leamington Spa and Tunbridge Wells.

Trevor Toms, Bittles Green Farm, Motcombe, Dorset, SP7 9NX. Tel. 01747-811978.

Underwood Kitchens, Lawn Farm Business Centre, Grendon, Underwood, Bucks, HP1 0QX. Tel. 01296-770043.

Tim Wood Furniture, 41 Ballantine Street, London, SW18 1AL. Tel. 0171-924 1511. By appointment only. Bespoke designer kitchens.

Zeyko, Tel. 01727-835500 for stockists. Eco-friendly German kitchen makers who use natural and re-cyclable materials.

COOKERS

AEG, Tel. 01753-872324 for stockists. Domestic and industrial-size cookers.

Aga brochure request line, Tel. 0345-125207.

Belling, Tel. 01709-579902 for stockists. Dual fuel or electric combinations.

Bradshaw Appliances, Tel. 01275-343000 for further details. Importers of American cookers including the Viking range.

Britannia, Tel. 01253-300663. Large double ovens, professional appearance but suitable for home use.

Flacon, Tel. 01324-554221 for stockists. Range includes six-ring gas cooker in professional steel finish.

Forneaux de France, Tel. 0181-232 8882 for stockists. Traditionally-styled Lacanche stoves with chic French styling.

Imperial, Tel. 01235-554488 for stockists. Professional-style domestic cookers with multi-functions.

Leisure, Tel. 01926-427027 for stockists. Large-scale Rangemaster cookers in a choice of two finishes.

Merloni Domestic Appliances, Tel. 01895-858200 for stockists. Ranges include Ariston electric ovens.

Nelson Catering Equipment, Tel. 0181-993 6198 for further details. Stockists of professional Garland & Wolf ranges.

Olis, Tel. 01455-272364 for stockists. Industrial cookers.

Rayburn, brochure request line, Tel. 0345-626147.

Rosieres, Tel. 0117-9381900. Large-scale domestic cookers including the Boscuse range.

Smeg, Tel. 01235-861090 for stockists. Domestic and professional ranges.

Viking, Tel. 01275-343000. Professional ranges with multi-function grills, etc.

FRIDGES

AEG, Tel. 01753-872101 for stockists for a range of fridges and freezers.

Alternative Plans, Tel. 0171-228 6460. Fridges by Boffi in sixteen colours.

Amana from NRC Bott, Tel. 01923 776464. CFC- and frost-free fridges.

American Appliance Centre, Tel. 0181-506 2039. Importers of large American fridges with integral cool drink and ice dispenser in the door.

Electrolux, customer careline, Tel. 01582-585858. Wide range of domestic fridges and freezers.

Forneaux de France, Tel. 0181-232 8882 for chic French fridges, including one with a glass panel door.

Smeg, Tel. 01235-861090 for stockists. American fridge-freezers in a choice of primary colours and stainless steel finishes.

SINKS, TAPS AND SURROUNDS

Blanco, Foster Beard, Oxgate Lane, London, NW2 7JN. Tel. 0181-450 9100. Stainless steel sinks and drainers.

Bordercraft, Old Forge, Peterchurch, Herefordshire, HR2 OSD. Tel. 01981-550251. Bespoke hardwood work-tops.

Brass & Traditional Sinks Ltd, Devauden Green,

93

Chepstow, Gwent, NP6 6PL. Tel. 01291-650738.
Classic and contemporary sinks.

Franke UK Ltd, Manchester International Office
Centre, Styal Road, Manchester, M22 5WB. Tel. 0161-
436 6280. Stainless steel and synthetic surround sinks
and draining boards.

The Granite Worktop Company, PO Box 195,
Bolton, BL7 OFB. For a free colour brochure Tel.
01204-852247.

WASTE DISPOSER

In-Sink-Erator Division, **Emerson Electric UK Ltd,**
Chelmsford Road, Great Dunmow, Essex, CM6 1LP.
Tel. 01371-873073.

DISHWASHERS AND WASHING MACHINES

AEG, Tel. 01753-872101.

Bosch, Tel. 0181-573 8888.

Hoover European Appliance Group, Tel. 01685
721222.

Miele, Tel. 01235 554455.

Smeg, Corinthian Court, 80 Milton Park, Abingdon,
Oxon, OX14 4RY. Tel. 01235-861090.

Zanussi, Tel. 01635 521313.

TILES

Ceramic Blue, 10 Blenheim Crescent, London, W11
1NN. Tel. 0171-727 0288.

Criterion Tiles, 196 Wandsworth Bridge Road,
London, SW6 2UF. Tel. 0171-736 9610.

Fired Earth, Twyford Mill, Oxford Road, Adderbury,
Oxon, OX17 3HP. Tel. 01295-812088 for further infor-
mation and nearest branch.

Marlborough Tiles, Elcot Lane, Marlborough, Wilts,
SN8 2AY. Tel. 01672-512422.

Paris Ceramics, 583 King's Road, London, SW6 2EH.
Tel. 0171-371 9666.

Reject Tile Shop, Tel. 0171-731 6098.

Worlds End Tiles, British Rail Yard, Silverthorne
Road, London, SW8 3HE. Tel. 0171-720 8358.

FLOORING

Amtico, 18 Hanover Square, London, W1A 9EA. Tel.
0171-629 6258, or nationwide 0800 667766.

Criterion Tiles, 196 Wandsworth Bridge Road,
London, SW6 2UF. Tel. 0171-736 9610. Ceramic tiles.

First Floor, 174 Wandsworth Bridge Road, London,
SW6 2UQ. Tel. 0171-736 1123. Industrial and heavy-
duty flooring as well as linoleum and vinyl.

Forbo-Nairn Ltd, PO Box 1, Den Road, Kirkcalldy,
Fife, KY1 2SB. Tel. 01592-643111.

Hardwood Flooring Co, 146-152 West End Lane,
West Hampstead, London, NW6 1SD. Tel. 0171-328
8481.

Junkers, Wheaton Road, Witham, Essex, CM8 3UJ.
Tel. 01376-517512.

Marley Floors Ltd, Dickley Lane, Lenham, Maidstone,
Kent, ME17 2DE. Tel. 01622-854000.

Sinclair Till, 793 Wandsworth Bridge Road, London,
SW8 3JQ. Tel. 0171-720 0031.

LIGHTING

Christopher Wray, 600 King's Road, London, SW6
2DX. Tel. 0171-736 8434.

John Cullen, 585 King's Road, London SW6 2EH. Tel.
0171-371 5400. Lighting advice and schemes, as well as
the latest in contemporary lighting techniques and
fittings.

McCloud, 269 Wandsworth Bridge Road, London,
SW6 2TX. Tel. 0171-371 7151.

Mr Light, 279 King's Road, London, SW3 5EW. Tel.
0171-352 7525.

RADIATORS

Bisque, 244 Belsize Road, London, NW6 4BT. Tel.
0171-328 2225. For details of other stockists call head
office at 15 Kingsmead Square, Bath, Avon, BA1 2AB.
Tel. 01225-469244.

Stiffkey, Stiffkey, Wells-next-the-Sea, Norfolk, NR23
1AJ. Tel. 01328-830084. Reconditioned and salvaged
radiators.

CURTAINS, SHUTTERS AND BLINDS

American Shutters, 72 Station Road, London, SW13 OLS. Tel. 0181-876 5905.

Lufaflex, for stockists, Tel. 01698-881281. Modern and traditional-style roller and slat blinds.

Plantation Shutters, 14 Marcus Terrace, London, SW18 2JW. Tel. 0181-870 7996 for further details and brochure.

Ruffle & Hook, Florence Works, 34½ Florence Street, London N1 2DT. Tel. 0171-226 0370. Curtains to order, simple styles of hessian and jute available.

The Shutter Shop, Queensbury House, Dilly Lane, Hartley Witney, Hants, RG27 8EQ. Tel. 01252-844575.

ACCESSORIES

Aero, 96 Westbourne Grove, London, W2 5RT. Tel. 0171-221 1950. Contemporary kitchen gadgets.

The Conran Shop, Michelin House, 81 Fulham Road, London, SW3 6RD. Tel. 0171-589 7401. Stylish designer pieces.

Designers' Guild, 267/271 & 177 King's Road, London, SW3 5EN. Tel. 0171-243 7300. Bright and colourful cloths and plates.

Divertimenti, 139/141 Fulham Road, London, SW3 5EN. Tel. 0171-581 8065. Beautiful china and a full range of kitchen gadgets and equipment.

Graham & Green, 7 Elgin Crescent, London, W11 2JA. Tel. 0171-727 4592. Wide range of china and glass.

Habitat, Tel. 0645-334433 for nearest branch. Wide range of standard and more unusual tableware and glass.

Jerry's Home Store, 163/167 Fulham Road, London, SW3 6SN. Tel. 0171-581 0909.

Liberty, 210/220 Regent Street, London, W1R 6AH. Tel. 0171-734 1234.

Muji, 26 Great Marlborough Street, London, W1V 1HL. Tel. 0171-494 1197. Ranges of air-tight containers, plus storage and Oriental accessories.

Summerhill & Bishop, 100 Portland Place, London, W11 4LN. Tel. 0171-221 4566. Wide range of kitchen accessories and gadgets.

USA

American Blind, 909 North Sheldon, Plymouth, MI 48170. Tel. 800 575 8014. Shutters and blinds.

American Olean, 1000 Cannon Avenue, Lansdale, PA 19446. Tel. 215 855 1111. Flooring.

American Standard, 1 Centennial Ave, Piscataway, NJ 08854. Tel. 800 524 9797. Sinks.

Armstrong, Box 3001, Lancaster, PA 17604. Tel. 800 704 8000. Flooring.

Bell Products, 722 Soscol Avenue, Napa, CA 94559. Tel. 707 255 1811. Radiators.

Brea Hardwoods, 6367 Eastland Road, Brook Park OH 44142. Tel. 216 234 7949. Flooring.

Bruce Hardwood Floors, Box 660100, Dallas, TX 75266. Tel. 800 722 4647. Flooring.

Congoleum Corp., PO Box 3127, 3705 Quaker Bridge Road, Mercerville, NJ 08619. Tel. 800 934 3567. Flooring.

Country Floors, 15 East 16th Street, New York, NY 10003. Tel. 212 267 8300. Tiles.

Crate & Barrel, 311 Gilmen Road, Wheeling, IL 60090. Tel. 800 323 5461. Accessories.

Fieldstone Cabinetry, PO Box 109, Northwood, IA 50459. Tel. 515 324 2114. Units.

Jenn-Air, 3035 Shadeland Ave, Indianapolis, IN 46226. Tel. 317 545 2271. Appliances.

Lightoller, 100 Lighting Way, Secaucus, NJ 07096. Tel. 800 628 8692. Lighting.

Pottery Barn, PO Box 7044, San Francisco, CA 94120. Tel. 800 922 5507. Accessories.

Sub-zero Freezer Co., PO Box 44130, Madison, WI 53744-4130. Tel. 800 200 7820. Appliances.

Viking Range Corporation, PO Box 956, Greenwood, MS 38930. Tel. 601 455 1200. Appliances.